The one about the (young) Nigerian poet in Nottingham who writes random poems about the random things he sees around the city, like shirtless men, playing children, or women reading books on the tram.

First Published 2017
by Big White Shed, Nottingham
ISBN 978-0-9933805-7-0
Copyright © Akor Opaluwah, 2017
A catalogue copy of this book is available from the British Library.
Printed and bound by Booksfactory EU.

Yinka said we should write for thirty days,
Wendy, Kamilah and Vanessa read over 2 years of rough poetry,
Anne said "nice, keep writing",
Chris said he liked them.

Thanks.

Preface

I spent a while writing short poems about things I saw and people I met while in Nottingham.

This collection explores the things I saw.

I hope you enjoy the path through which my mind constantly travels and the (relatively) inconsequential moments I enjoy sighting.

Grace_&_Peace.

1.

The one about my dear friend who was deeply in love and longed for her heart to find rest again.

Butterflies
are still beautiful
to behold.

Your smile
is beautiful.

2.

The one about the night we had a Monologue Session and Cleo told a story while sat between candles, silence, awe, and hearts, trapped in her sincerity.

Hussssh!!!!
You loud beating heart.

Do not break open,
the tranquil. Or
the chains.

3.

The one about the guy in a black leather jacket sitting at the far right corner of the night bus.

Loneliness
has a smell.

Solemn.

4.

**The one about
the ex-traveller
and exciting
physiotherapist
I met on the train
from Coventry
who loved
badminton,
potato farms
in Australia,
and saw the
world
in colours.**

Stretch the world
over the seas and pain.

Those fields, by modest adventures,
are covered with your smile.

5.

The one about some random phrases that I wrote down and could not remember the chain of thought that led to them but decided they could start interesting political or societal analysis discussions and so slipped them into my book.

Choice is freedom.
Time is not data.

We expect more
from technology

and less
from each other.

6.

The one about the girl in a red jacket with golden hair that flowed like an unending waterfall.

Would your company
forever be a well-crafted
scene trapped in the
cacophony of
an imagination?

~mine~

7.

**The one about
the guy
with brightly
coloured hair
who laughed
hysterically
to the voice
across his
two-way radio.**

~contagious~

His laughter.
Highly contagious.

~contagious~

8.

The one about the ex-teacher, now chef who had a desirable music collection, and the warm-hearted angel who welcomed me from the bus at Norwich.

They served
blessings spiced with
anchovies, black olives, cheese
and a side of salmon.

I smiled in Spanish,
spoke in full,
thanked in [great] joy
and slept
with a smile.

9.

The one about the Sofa Sound Nottingham guest artist with blonde hair and a voice that rode the caves and cracked the rocks.

Whispers,
screams, soul, and
melody.

Can the evening gift a tired heart
finer respite that soothes better
than songs from
a Sofa?

sigh

10.

The one about Paloma; the Poetercize interpretive dancer at the Nottingham Poetry Festival who painted poems with her body.

Through different postures,
she smiled as the cheers radiated
off her aura.

Heaven seems human
today.

11.

**The one about
the guy
in a red hat,
grey sleeveless
jumper and
shorts on a
cold
British
evening.**

Corked lips,
bright sneakers
and stifled laugh.

I wonder the joke that crawled
from his shoe laces.

12.

The one about the swimming instructor at John Carroll Leisure Centre who was in a wheelchair.

Some rocks
are just too heavy
for life to sink.

The red tree
with the grand wings
has no fear of the hurricane.

Life.

13.

**The one about
the day
I played
basketball
for two hours
even though I had
not done any real
body straining
exercise in about
three years.**

Seventy five
came real fast.
Lower back feels like
the host of a river dance festival
performed by sumo wrestlers.

It hurt like I was seventy
and five years
old.

I am scared of growing old.

14.

The one about my friend who said she was "off to bed with a joy filled heart" after a lovely evening with drinks, cards and loud laughs that reverberated on the stars and choruses of the group of lads that started singing 'Angels' by Robbie Williams beside us.

Plant a smile
as you sink beneath
the cloak with slumber.

The flowers that sprout
en la mañana
are what we refer to
when we whisper
beauty.

15.

The one about
the night
people and
the little pleasure
that they
share even
though they
are
usually unaware
of the similarities
in them or the
synchronisation
of their actions.

Two strangers
one seated
one stood, leaning on the pillar.
Bus shelters on both street sides
draped in night light.

Two strangers
yawned simultaneously.

The world smiled.
Simple pleasures.

16.

The one about the girl who was so in love with her ex even in his rejection she poured her heart out in the almost spherical shape of tears on a coffee table in hopes that he would paddle back to her.

Can a rock be drowned?
Or a seed be grown?
Or the sky be lassoed?
Or sunrise be welcomed?

She searched
for the true
and impossible.

All
plus more,
she gifted
for his sail to change course.

This silence
kills (me) the spectator.

17.

The one about
the girl
who sat
with arms crossed
and
smile
abated.

Joy was a pendulum
Its swing finds you.
Periodically.

Joy was a pendulum.
It found sync
when she sat with you.

Time stopped away joy.

Broken pendulum.

18.

**The one about
the Poetry is Dead
Good poet
with pink shoes,
green hair
and poetic
excitement.**

These shoes can only be worn
by someone who has
walked
on sunshine.

The residue brightens up her life
our lives
her poetry.

~singing~
I'm walking on sunshine.

19.

The one about Chris McLoughlin and his poem at the Big White Shed poetry night held at Debbie Bryan's beautiful cafe in Nottingham.

His poems
told me to look again
at life
and its stillness.

There is still room
to breathe.

20.

The one about the moment where the 34 bus pulled up while the 43 bus drove by on the same street.

Reality
may have thought it funny
to place my consciousness
along with seeming
opposites.

~giggle~

It was funny.
Amusing.

21.

**The one about
the lady
standing on
the tram
wearing
a bright flowery
dress and
reading a book
while the tram
whizzed by me.
Standing.**

Enchantment.
She travelled two journeys
simultaneously.

She reached two worlds
simultaneously.

22.

**The one about
the lady
in a
black
Disciple shirt,
red skirt,
and carrying
two bags.**

Two smiles blossomed.
They were watered by kindness,
kind words and patience.

She spent a moment
speaking with him.

He spent a moment
speaking with her.

She stood.
He sat.
On the street.

~conversation continues
under the British summer~

23.

The one about the man in a suit in a suit with a well-groomed beard and sunglasses, who had two bags slung over his shoulder.

Everyone
should carry two bags.

It felt most appropriate
to think of that
over the mind tasking
story I had involuntarily started
grafting as to why
he would be with
two bags slung over his shoulders.

Everyone should carry two bags;
a back pack and a shoulder bag.

That is my rule.

24.

**The one about
the conversation
I had with a friend
about rules
and the
importance
of spontaneous
travel
across Europe.**

Rule number two!

Everyone should travel to Germany
to have lunch there.

"And then what?"

Return to Nottingham.

25.

**The one about
the guy
in the light
green jacket
and pastel orange
shirt
taking a slow walk
towards
the bus stop.**

Sadness was the floor board
that adorned his house

"I can cry at any time.
That saddens me".

He tried.
He succeeded.
He walked on.

26.

The one about those two bikes I always see leaning on the wall in the parking garage of the Study Inn luxury accommodation down on Clarendon Street in Nottingham.

Move!
Go out.
Let me miss you.
Grow some balls and move.
Horses would not stand for this.

Move!

27.

**The one about
a shirtless guy
with bright
orange
trousers
doing a wheelie
around the
Old Market Square
on a rather calm,
warm and
sunny evening.**

Bikes were made with two wheels
for a good reason.

Wheelies and walking sticks
that find home within spinning bicycle spokes
are not the best of friends.

So I hear
from the guy with the bloodied palm
and ruined bike.

28.

The one about
the girl with green
hair sitting at
the Peveril Street
bus stop
under the
only working
light.

Her cloak
seemed coloured
in loneliness

...seemed.

I didn't ask.

29.

**The one about
the time
where I went
to play basketball
and then twisted
my ankle about
twenty minutes
into the first
game.**

"Limp?
This is how I walk
you straight walking homo sapiens"

said the insufferable
denier.

30.

**The one about
the line
in the song,
'The One With
My Friends'
by Marty
where he said
"I wrote that line
on a plane."**

Did he?
Proof?

I need this.

31.

**The one about
my co-worker
who had travelled
the world
for a while
before taking a
break for
a while.**

You have tasted the earth
brushed your teeth
with gold and white sand
and drank the clouds.

No wonder
your smile looks
like the sun.

32.

**The one about
the time
where I had
to wear an Aircast
on my left foot
after I had
broken my
little metatarsal.**

Three legs
aren't that efficient.

The multitude
holds the kid and
his sprint is lost
in the excess.

33.

**The one about
the lady in white
and black
sat outside
TK Maxx
whom I saw
smoking
on a warm evening
from my seat
in Nero cafe.**

I always wonder.
Do cigarettes slow the passing of time?
Does the smoke
settle like a bubble
and swallow its conduit
in a silence from the world?

Inhale.
Hold.
Stare at cigarette.
Exhale.

34.

**The one about
the man on
the 77 bus
from Strelley
who I locked
eyes with
for about three
seconds
(not weird at all).**

I have heard
life is a cruel banker.
Unpredictable.

Not all dues
are paid back to the
tenacious.

I heard
life is a mean ol' banker.

Hoarder.

35.

The one about the student whose umbrella tore into two as soon as it was courted by the over-enthusiastic wind that accompanied a gentle drizzle.

Your laughter
is the warm sun
this shower needs.

Heaven
cries rain.

Earth
laughs sun.

36.

The one about the hug I saw rise from a distance and had to wait for almost an eternity to see how it would conclude even though I never really thought there would be any difference in this hug from the millions of hugs I had seen and/or partaken in.

I hope you will catch me.
I have faith you will catch me.
I love it that you will catch me.

The exhilarating moment
between the leap
and the hug.

37.

The one about the expert tip on how to finish a Rubik's Cube we found at Joel's house when he had his rather interesting birthday celebration where he wore a shirt with his picture on it.

"Paint it all red
and you will never get it wrong."

"Can I drink that paint?"
I thought.

38.

The one about the Sofa Sound artist from New Zealand whose song shut my eyes and told me of failure and train engines through beautiful sounds that tasted like dry white wine and cheese on an evening clouded with friends, jokes and laughter.

We are all
like you.

We are not
like you.

We are.
You.

~smile~
~exhale~
~smile~

39.

The one about the girl whose voice was so soft that I was certain if she had stopped mid-sentence and said "let us get married" I would have dropped life and been at the altar with her faster than any other rash decision any human had ever made.

Her voice
felt like clouds.

She could speak
to warring countries
and in the fewest sentences
turn the battle front
to a baking meetup.

We
would have
too many cakes.

Enough
for all the soldiers.

And peace.

40.

**The one about
the old man
with a grey
ponytail hopping
with both hands
in the air
after who
I supposed was his
granddaughter
(or great
granddaughter)
while they crossed
Market Square.**

I saw time
do a dance
and smile. Excitement
was tucked in blue
pullover and pink dress.
Simultaneously.

Time was mirrored.
And time loved it.

Hop.
Hop.
Hop.

41.

The one about the shirtless guy with a small bag slung over his shoulder while he kicked a football high into the air.

Your vibrancy
is the pleasure of
the orange evening.

Even the sun
leans closer to
taste of your joy

Thanks.

42.

The one about the girl in white who walked in front of the black car that gently inched a little close to her before the driver roared his engine, accentuated by a whiney car horn, both of which startled her to stop, turn and point a smile at the driver.

Once,
It was rumoured
that love when painted on a heart,
pitches its conspicuously luminous
bright orange tent
on a face.

Today,
I found the evidence.

43.

The one about the guy in a black jacket who was walking about smiling but continually fought to hold the tears inside.

He feels like
a beaver, bad at his job.

A weak dam constantly
needs to be held closed.

Tight.
In place.

By weak limbs and
frivolous excuses.

44.

The one about the friend who I could talk to with ease about the entirety of life and knowledge and still not feel bored even after lifetimes of extended conversations.

We have
travelled through
earth, ideas, knowledge,
civilization.

Sit with me
for two moments
more.

45.

**The one about
the guy who kept
checking his watch
at Jam Café
while he talked
to the lady
in black who
looked equally as
interested in the
conversation as
he seemed.**

Why hath thou
put thyself
in this predicament
on a night, so pleasant
as this?

~I assumed he thought
in old English~

46.

**The one about
the Mouthy Poet
who strings
spoken
words over guitar
that held the
room in silence
till our hearts
and widened eyes
were floated
by tears.**

Through words, and
melody.

Again, you, through words
and serene melody,
showed my heart
what beautiful awe
looks like.

Again.

47.

The one about the girl with the crutch and smiling eyes.

Not even a limp,
the grey, or rain
could dampen
the smile.

... sunshine.

48.

**The one about
the day
when almost
all my students
and I had a cold
and so we were
sniffing, sneezing
and holding our
woozy heads
all through
the class.**

The orchestra of breathing
was not a pleasure
for its audience.

sniff
strong sniff
sniff

Light heads, cloudy eyes,
and full bellies.

This poem is about
something quite
disgusting.

49.

**The one about
the new friend
on Facebook
whose art,
writing,
and pictures
were intriguing.**

Red lips
and a word-laden
strut.

There is an avalanche
of understanding oozing
from her confidence.

j

50.

**The one about
the girl
whose art
lived on the
peripheral of my
philosophy which
seemed
encompassing
prior to our
encounter.**

How can
the vastness;
that which has lingered
in darkness, wake to a Saturday
morning light. One so
bright and colourful.

Write for me.
Again.

Please.

51.

The one about
the lady
swaddled in a
bright red scarf
while on
the tram
that passed
by my window
as I sat, staring
out of Starbucks
beside the Old
Market Square.

She wore colours
that spoke of a beauty
full world.

52.

The one about the lady in a blue dress, gold chain, keyboard and a voice that calmed the enchanted room.

Drive!
She sang. To the still air
and awe of the room.

From a sofa
the night serenades
rough waters.

And the hearts that burned,
the cool of the evening
is calmed by solitude.

53.

**The one about
that friend
who I never
could meet with
because
our lives
inexplicably
seemed to have
a predisposition
for not
aligning.**

We are
the seasons.

Running after each other
unto each other
by each other.

Never colliding.

54.

**The one about
the bright
bouquet of flowers
that lifted
my mood
even though
I had only seen
a picture of them
as they were given
to Kamilah
who was in
London.**

I never knew
flowers had really strong
wings.

These ones
lifted my arched shoulders,
curved my lips upward,
and filled the air
with summer.

sniff

Feet dangling in the air
toes wiggling in excitement.

The one about

55.

The one about...